HUMAN BODY

Written by Steve Parker

Illustrations by Meme design & Stephen Sweet

TOP THAT

Licensed exclusively to Top That Publishing Ltd
Tide Mill Way, Woodbridge, Suffolk, IP12 1AP, UK
www.topthatpublishing.com
Copyright © 2014 Tide Mill Media
0 2 4 6 8 9 7 5 3 1
Printed and bound in China

THE BRAIN IS BOSS

The brain is in charge of almost everything the body does. Actions we rarely think about, such as breathing and making the heart beat, are controlled by the brain. Even when we sleep, the brain is still busy – especially when we dream.

What is the brain

The brain may look like a blob of jelly, but it is one of the most extraordinary and amazing creations in the universe. It is home to a staggering one hundred billion nerve cells, or neurons! The brain is the site of your thoughts, memories and hopes. It monitors and regulates unconscious bodily processes like heart rate and breathing, and coordinates almost every movement you make.

Are human brains different to animal brains

Human brains may not be the biggest or heaviest brains in the animal kingdom, but they are certainly the most complex. Tucked inside your head is a brain that has evolved over millions of years to become the most advanced body part in the world! Each neuron in your brain can make contact with tens of thousands of others, via tiny structures called synapses. Our brains form over one million new connections every single second! These connections are constantly changing and no two brains are alike.

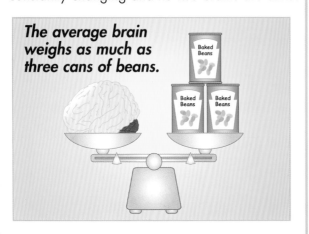

The average brain weighs as much as three cans of beans.

The human brain.

cerebellum

brain stem

spinal cord

sight centre

What do the brain parts do

The lower part, the brain stem, deals with vital body processes we rarely think about, like breathing, heartbeat and digesting food.
The smaller, wrinkled part at the lower rear, the cerebellum, is mainly for controlling muscles and making skilled and coordinated movements.
The large upper part, the cerebrum, receives information from the eyes, ears and other senses, and carries out thinking and speaking processes.

When we sleep, does the brain stop working

No way – in fact it's very busy! Recordings of its tiny electrical nerve signals, or 'brain waves', by a medical EEG (electroencephalograph) machine, show the brain stays active even during sleep, and especially when dreaming. New research shows that the sleeping brain may be sorting out recent events and memories, and deciding which ones to keep.

Why are some people left-handed

No one really knows – but we do know that the right side of the brain controls the left side of the body, including the left hand, while the brain's left side controls the body's right side. In most people, one or other of the brain's sides is in charge, or dominant. In about eleven people in every 100, the brain's right side is dominant so they use their left hand most.

FACT BYTES

Every part of the body is made of microscopic parts called cells, and the brain has more than 500 billion of them!

On average, a slightly higher proportion of left-handed people are likely to be creative or artistic in some way, such as musicians, painters or sculptors, compared to right-handed people.

cerebrum

touch and sensation

taste centre

basic movements

planning movements

balance centre

speech centre

frontal lobe is involved in awareness and personality

hearing centre

ellum controls
ment, posture
alance

How the brain works.

LOOK HERE!

From the moment you wake up in the morning until the moment you go to sleep, your eyes are gathering information and sending it to your brain to be interpreted. Your eyes are delicate and precious. They should be shielded from sunlight and protected from harm during dangerous activities like sport.

How does the eye work ?

As the light from an object that you are looking at passes through the lens in your eye, the image becomes reversed (turned backwards) and inverted (turned upside-down). At the retina, light-sensitive nerve cells send electrical messages along the optic nerve to the brain where information about the image is processed and understood.

Upside-down view.

lens
iris
pupil
conjunctiva
cornea
sclera
choroid
eye-moving mus

Why are eyes coloured ?

Eye colour is determined by the levels of a molecule called melanin present in the coloured tissue of the iris. The levels of melanin, in turn, are determined by genes inherited from parents. Brown is the most common eye colour in the world. Blue eyes are rarer than any other eye colour, and often found in people from Europe.

parents' eye colour

proportion of eye colour in children

 + = **or**

 + = **or**

 + = **or**

Why people can't see in the dark ?

When light fades, the cone cells of the retina (those responsible for processing colour) are no longer able to work effectively. At this time, rod cells (responsible for processing light) process any available light as shades of grey (monochrome). In this way, the human eye is less effective when it gets darker. The brain recognises the shades of grey processed by the rod cells as 'darkness'.

retina

fovea (yellow spot, area of most detailed vision)

optic nerve

blood vessels at centre of optic nerve

blood vessels branch out over surface of retina

FACT BYTES

Cone cells detect only three colours of light – red, green and blue.

All the thousands of colours we see are combinations of these three basic, or primary, colours.

Each day the eyeball makes more than 60,000 movements as it looks around, up and down.

How often do we blink ?

We blink, on average, about once every two or three seconds. However, it depends greatly on the amount of dust floating in the air, whether it is windy, and many other conditions. Each blink lasts about one-fifth of a second, which means that through the daytime we have our eyes closed for a total of about an hour!

What do our eyelids do ?

Eyelids keep our eyes from drying out and prevent dirt from entering and irritating them. The rims of the human eyelid are lined with oil-producing glands. When the eye blinks, the oil from these glands is spread across the eye, ensuring that it remains moist.

Meanwhile, eyelashes serve as 'dust-catchers', catching irritants before they enter the eye.

Why do pupils change in size ?

The coloured ring of the eye, known as the iris, tightens and relaxes, letting the appropriate amount of light pass through the hole in the centre, called the pupil. Inside, the brightness of the light is detected by the retina, which sends messages to the brain so that it can continually adjust the iris muscles.

Close-up of the retina.

cone cell

rod cell

network of nerve cells

nerve fibres to optic nerve

LOOK HERE!

WHAT'S THAT SMELL?

A beautiful cake fresh from the oven. Flowers during spring. A pile of dirty clothes. How do you smell these smells and thousands more? It's your nose of course! Let's be a little bit nosy and find out more about this incredible organ!

Why do we 'get used' to strong smells ❓

If we detect a strong odour in a place, and keep on detecting it for a long time, we might become distracted and miss other smells which could be important too. After a time, therefore, the brain ignores a strong, but constant, smell and concentrates on other, new ones. In fact, most of the body's senses do this. In a windblown place the ears detect the noisy wind at first, but after a time, we no longer notice it. Becoming used to what the senses receive like this is called habituation.

How do people smell things ❓

A smell is made of airborne particles called 'odorants', which touch two patches in the nose when we breathe in air. The odorants land on micro-hairs called 'cilia'. When this happens, a series of tiny nerve signals are sent to the brain and that's when we get the smell.

cilia

air flows into nose

odorants

air space (sinus) in skull bone

cartilage (gristle) of nose

air chamber inside nose

nostril

palate (roof of mouth)

lip

tooth

tongue

jaw bone

hyoid

Why is smell so important ❓

Identifying smells is your brain's way of telling you about (or helping you to make 'scents' of) your environment. Have you ever smelt smoke from a fire? Instantly, your brain interpreted the smell as a sign of danger and you knew to check where the smell was coming from. Your sense of smell can also warn you not to eat something that smells rotten, like sour milk or mouldy bread.

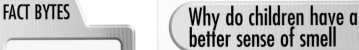

Inside the nose and mouth.

cilia

olfactory bulb
pre-sorts nerve signals

olfactory
nerve to
brain

Why do children have a better sense of smell

As people age, the cilia inside the nasal cavity become fewer. This means that young people, generally, have a far better sense of smell than older people. A similar thing happens with the taste buds in the mouth. Younger people experience smell and taste more strongly than older people do.

How does smell affect the taste of food

You may think of the tongue when you think about taste – but you couldn't taste anything without some help from the nose! The ability to smell and taste go together because odours from foods allow us to taste more fully.

To understand how smell enhances flavour, take a bite of food and see how it tastes. Then pinch your nose and take another bite. You should notice that without smell, food tastes more bland. When you have a bad cold you may temporarily lose your sense of smell. Although your taste buds continue to work, the food you eat will taste of very little.

tonsil

back-
bones
in
neck

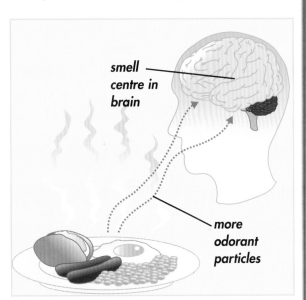

smell
centre in
brain

more
odorant
particles

WHAT'S THAT SMELL?

SMILE A WHILE

Your mouth is a remarkable thing. Your teeth tear up food, munching it into a wet ball. Chemicals in your saliva moisten the food, releasing its wonderful flavours. Your tongue pushes the ball of chewed food to the back of your throat, and then it is gone ...

How does the tongue taste ?

Most taste buds are located around the sides and across the back of your tongue. They provide information about the taste of the food you eat. When your taste buds come into contact with food, they send nerve signals to the brain, where they can be interpreted as tastes you may recognise.

Why do some foods taste bitter ?

bitter

sour

salty

sweet

The taste buds on the tongue's tip sense sweet flavours best. Those along the front sides detect salty ones, while sour flavours are detected along the rear sides. The taste buds across the back detect bitter flavourants. Therefore, we taste something bitter last of all, usually just as, and after, we swallow.

How many teeth do we have

More than 50 – but not all at once! A typical youngster has 20 baby, or milk, teeth which appear from front to back, from about the age of six months to three years. By about six years these first teeth start to fall out naturally and the 32 adult, or permanent, teeth begin to grow, again appearing from front to back. The rearmost cheek, or 'wisdom', teeth come through at 16–20 years of age, but in some people, they never develop.

frontalis muscle raises your eyebrows in surprise

temporalis muscle helps to close mouth when chewing

orbicularis oculi muscles in eyelids make them blink

zygomaticus muscle pulls mouth wide to smile

masseter muscle closes jaws for chewing

orbicularis oris muscles of lips close to keep in foods and drinks

Under the skin and inside the mouth are plenty of muscles, including the lips and tongue.

Why are teeth shaped differently

The teeth in your mouth are different sizes and shapes. This is because they perform specific jobs. At the front of the mouth are two front teeth called incisors. They are straight-edged and sharp to bite off and slice up chunks of food. Next to them is a taller, more pointed canine, which is better for tearing and pulling. Then come two premolars and three molars, which are wide with broad tops, for powerful chewing and crushing.

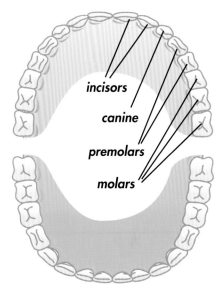

incisors

canine

premolars

molars

Both the upper and lower sets have the same number of tooth types.

premolar tooth

canine tooth

incisor teeth

FACT 'BITE' BYTES

The tongue is almost all muscle, with a thin, taste-sensitive covering. In fact it's the most flexible muscle in the body, formed from six pairs of smaller, or intrinsic, muscles all joined and working together.

The enamel covering a tooth is the hardest substance in the body. A typical tooth bites and chews over 15 million times through its life.

Each day six parts around the mouth (called salivary glands) make about one-and-a-half litres of saliva, or spit, to make food soft when chewing and easy to swallow.

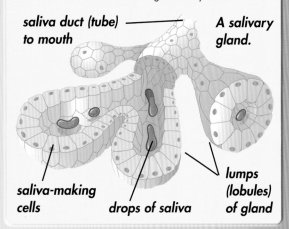

saliva duct (tube) to mouth

A salivary gland.

saliva-making cells

drops of saliva

lumps (lobules) of gland

FEELING HAIRY?

Humans are one of the hairiest creatures on Earth! Every part of your body – except for your lips, palms of your hands and soles of your feet – is covered by hair. By adulthood, you're likely to have about 5 million hairs poking out of your skin – about the same number as a gorilla!

Why do we have hair ?

Hair keeps us warm, protects the body and helps us to make sense of the world around us. When a person is cold or in danger, hair is likely to stand on end, trapping heat and making us look bigger. Hair can also help keep dust out of the eyes, ears and nose.

Why does hair turn grey ?

Older people tend to develop grey hair because the pigment in the hair disappears and the hair turns colourless. The grey or white appearance of an individual hair is the result of the absence of something called melanin, the same stuff responsible for eye colour. A head of hair will appear grey as a result of the combination of coloured and colourless hair – not because it is actually grey.

sebaceous gland

nerve endings

A hair follicle.

sebaceous gland

nerve endings

hair root

growing point of hair

Why is some hair curly ?

Whether your hair is straight, wavy or curly depends on the shape of your hair shaft. A round hair shaft produces very straight hair. When the hair shaft is oval it produces wavy or curly hair. Really curly hair is produced by flattened or kidney-shaped hair shafts. The amount of moisture in the air can alter the curliness of hair, when water is forced back into the hair fibre.

Human hair is not smooth but 'scaly' at 900 times magnification!

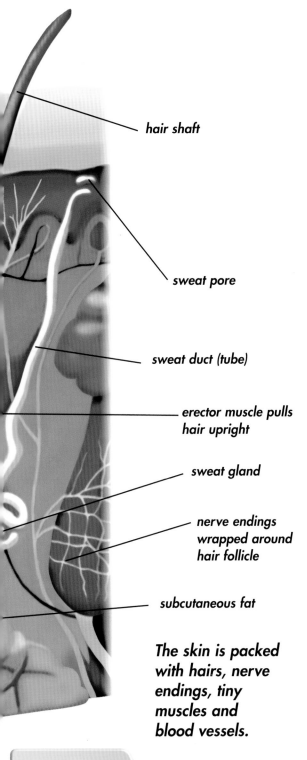

hair shaft

sweat pore

sweat duct (tube)

erector muscle pulls hair upright

sweat gland

nerve endings wrapped around hair follicle

subcutaneous fat

The skin is packed with hairs, nerve endings, tiny muscles and blood vessels.

FACT BYTES

Nails are made of the same substance as hair, called keratin.

An eyebrow or eyelash hair lasts for only 10 weeks.

Hairs on the head grow about 12 mm each month, although fine, fair hair grows more slowly than thick, dark hair.

How many hairs are on the head ?

The average human head has about 100,000 hairs. However, this number varies with age and hair colour. People with blonde hair have around 130,000 head hairs, brown haired people about 110,000 and red heads about 90,000. Older people usually have fewer hairs on their head than young adults do.

Why are men hairier ?

It's partly to do with inherited genes and also with the male hormone testosterone. Men grow long, thick facial hair which

forms the moustache and beard. Most women do have these hairs, and all the others that men have too – it's just that their hairs are mostly tiny and hardly visible.

WHAT AN EARFUL!

Not only is the ear the sense organ that detects sounds, it also plays a major role in the sense of balance and body position. The ear is a very complex organ that is divided into three parts: the outer ear, middle ear and inner ear.

How does the ear work

Sound waves travel down the ear tube, or canal, to a small sheet of thin skin called the eardrum. The eardrum vibrates as sound waves hit it. It passes its vibrations along three tiny bones, or ossicles – the malleus (hammer), incus (anvil) and stapes (stirrup) – to a part of the ear shaped like a snail and as big as a grape. This is the cochlea, in the inner ear. It is deep in the head, just behind the eye. The cochlea turns the vibrations into nerve signals and sends them along the auditory nerve to the brain.

FACT BYTES

The highest-pitched sounds which most people can hear are 20,000 vibrations per second – but a bat can hear sounds ten times higher.

The lowest-pitched sounds which most people can hear are 25–30 vibrations per second – but an elephant can hear sounds five times lower.

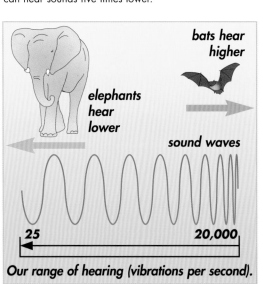

elephants hear lower

bats hear higher

sound waves

25   20,000

Our range of hearing (vibrations per second).

bony canal

pinna (outer ear flap)

cartilage (gristle) inside ear

ear lobe

bone of skull

How do ears affect balance

The ear is one of several organs responsible for maintaining the body's sense of balance. The ears, eyes, joints, skin and muscles all provide the brain with the information it needs to keep the body upright and balanced.

The parts of the ear responsible for balance are located in the inner ear – the utricle, the saccule and the semi-circular canals. When the body moves, the fluid in these tubes interacts with hair-like cells, which fire messages along nerves to the brain.

semi-circular canals
(for balance)

malleus
(hammer)

incus (anvil)

stapes (stirrup)

cochlea

cochlea nerve
to brain

*The delicate parts
of the inner ear are
protected by skull
bone around them.*

bone of skull

ardrum

eustachian
tube to throat

Why do we get ear wax ?

The lining of the ear canal continually makes small amounts of sticky wax called cerumen. This wax plays an important role in the cleaning of the ear canal. It also helps prevent dirt, bacteria, fungi and tiny insects from reaching and harming the eardrum. Hairs grow in the ear canal for the same reason, to keep things out. Excess ear wax can press against the ear drum or block the bony canal, which causes hearing to become impaired.

Why can't old people hear as well as young people ?

Older people tend to hear less well. In particular, they hear short, high-pitched sounds like 'ssss' and 't' less well, which makes it difficult to understand speech. They sometimes use hearing aids to help them.

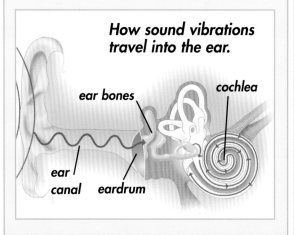

A hearing aid magnifies sounds.

What do we actually hear ?

We actually hear sound waves that are produced by the vibrations of air molecules. The size of these waves determines the loudness of the sound, which is measured in decibels (dB). The frequency of these waves determines the pitch of the sound, which is measured in hertz (Hz). In healthy adults, the ear is most sensitive to sounds in the middle range of 500 to 4,000 Hz.

*How sound vibrations
travel into the ear.*

ear bones

cochlea

ear
canal

eardrum

WHAT AN EARFUL!

THE SKELETON

Designed to provide maximum strength and mobility, the skeleton is the support network of the body, giving you shape and protecting your organs. Each bone is shaped to do a specific job and, where more flexibility is required, cartilage, ligaments and joints perform important functions.

Why do we need a skeleton

The skeleton provides a cage to protect the delicate parts of the body, while still allowing us to move. The ribcage, for instance, protects the lungs, heart, liver and stomach, while allowing the chest to expand and contract as we breathe. The skeleton is also the stable frame on which the other parts of the body are hung and supported.

The skull protects the brain.

How do joints work

When two or more bones in your body meet, they make a joint. Joints are divided into two types: mobile (synovial) and fixed (fibrous). Synovial joints include knees, shoulders and elbows. Here, two bones are held together by ligaments, which keep them in place as the muscles make the joint move. In fibrous joints, like the joints found in your skull, are bones that are joined by tough, stringy tissue, which allows very little or no movement.

Ball-and-socket joint.

shoulder joint

rounded head fits in cup-like cavity

Hinge joint

joint moves to and fro

elbow joint

How long do broken bones take to heal

Broken bones take a varying amount of time to heal, depending on the bone broken, the age of the person and the type of break. In children, small bones take about four weeks to heal. In adults, larger bones, such as the thigh bone (femur), can take up to three months. Complicated breaks take even longer to heal.

Which knee has an artificial joint?

skull

lower jaw

ball-and-socket joint

upper arm bone (humerus)

llarbone avicle)

stbone num)

ge

hinge joint

spinal bones (backbones)

hip bone (pelvis)

s

base of spine (sacrum)

kneecap (patella)

wrist bones (carpals)

thighbone (femur)

bone (tibia)

bone (fibula)

foot bones (metatarsals)

ankle bones (tarsals)

toe bones (phalanges)

How many bones are there in the body ?

Most adults have 206 in their body. However, about one person in 20 has an extra pair of ribs (13 pairs rather than 12). A newborn baby actually has more bones than an adult – around 350 at birth. Some of these bones fuse together as the child grows older.

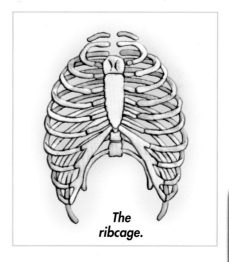

The ribcage.

FACT BYTES

baby   child

fontanelle

A baby is born with gaps in its skull, called fontanelles, which ensure that the skull is flexible enough to cope with birth.

A baby's skull does not form completely for up to two years. It looks like a jigsaw puzzle that joins together.

THE SKELETON

MUSCLE POWER

Did you know that you have more than 600 muscles in your body? They make every movement in your body possible, from the blink of an eye to a wave.

What does muscle do ?

Muscles move you! You have three different types of muscle in your body: skeletal muscle, smooth muscle and cardiac muscle. Skeletal muscle is attached to your bones. It enables you to consciously control most of your body, meaning that you can run, jump or walk as you choose. Smooth muscle is involuntary, which means that your brain tells it what to do without you thinking about it. It helps to move blood through your blood vessels and food through your digestive system. Cardiac muscle is found in the heart. This muscle is responsible for pushing blood around your body.

bicep

pectoralis major

abdominals hold in the soft parts, especially the intestines (guts).

How do muscles actually work ?

bicep

tricep

The bicep relaxes and the tricep contracts to extend the arm.

bicep

tricep

The bicep contracts and the tricep relaxes to bend the arm.

It all starts with orders from the brain. Special cells called neurons carry electrical messages from the brain through the nervous system to the muscles you want to move. Skeletal muscles work in pairs. When one muscle contracts (gets shorter) the other muscle must relax (get longer). If this relationship did not exist and both muscle groups were to contract at the same time, your arm would lock and there would be no movement at all.

sartorius

rectus femor

gastrocnemi

FACT BYTES

The sartorius is the body's longest muscle and runs from the side of the hip, down across the front of the thigh, to the inner knee.

The stapedius, deep in the ear, is the smallest muscle. It tightens to stop the stirrup ear bone moving too much and protects the delicate inner ear from damage by extra-loud sounds.

The gastrocnemius is the main calf muscle. It joins at its lower end to the heel bone by the body's thickest tendon, the Achilles.

What are muscles made of ❓

Tens of thousands of small fibres make up each muscle. Each fibre is made up of long thin cells, called myofibril, which are packed in bundles. Each muscle has lots of these bundles – the bigger the muscle the more bundles of fibres it has. Skeletal muscles are made up of fibres that have horizontal stripes when viewed under a microscope. Smooth muscle consists of more loosely arranged fibres. Cardiac muscle consists of fibres arranged in a neat criss-cross pattern.

tricep

deltoid

gluteus maximus

Achilles tendon

vastus

tibialis

toe-curling muscles (flexors)

toe-pointing muscles (extensors)

muscle sheath

bundles of muscle fibres

muscle fibres (myofibres)

myofibril consists of actin and myosin

blood vessels and nerves inside muscle

muscle fibre is a bundle of myofibrils

How many muscles does it take to smile or frown ❓

The face and head have more than 100 muscles, and we use them to make our vast range of facial expressions. It takes about 20 muscles to smile, but twice as many to frown. Scientists believe that our faces are pre-programmed to smile. A smile is used as a way of communicating with others, as a display of happiness or embarrassment.

MUSCLE POWER

THE SKIN YOU'RE IN

Your skin is alive! The largest organ in the human body, it's made up of many thin layers of cells in which you'll find nerves, blood vessels, hair follicles, glands and sensory receptors.

Why do we have skin

Your skin doesn't just cover you. It does much more. It offers protection from the world around you, including germs and dirt. It keeps unwanted water out and keeps your body's fluids and salts in. The skin contains a variety 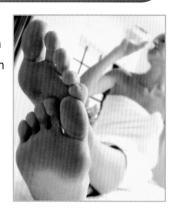 of nerve endings that react to temperature, touch, pressure, vibration and tissue damage. It also allows the body to keep cool through sweating and softens the impact of all kinds of wear and tear.

Why do some people get sunburnt more easily

Sunburn is a burn to the skin produced by too much exposure to ultraviolet (UV light), usually from the sun. It occurs when the melanin in the skin is not able to offer enough protection against UV light. Some people have lots of melanin and others have little. People with less melanin are more likely to become sunburnt.

UV rays get through   UV rays blocked

horny layer

germ layer
of epidermis

melanin

pigment forming
cells (melanocytes)

UV rays penetrate the layers of our skin.

Inside the skin are millions of nerve endings for touch.

hair shaft

sebaceous gland

sweat duct

nerve fibre

sweat gland

subcutaneous fat

FACT BYTES

If all of the coiled sweat glands from one body were straightened and joined end to end, they would stretch 50 kilometres.

The outer layer of skin rubs and wears away all the time as we move, wash, use towels and change clothes – and replaces itself entirely every month.

horny layer of dermis

middle layer of dermis

germ layer of dermis

nerve ending for heat, cold and pain

tiny blood vessels

nerve ending for light touch

erector muscle pulls hair upright

nerve endings

nerve fibres to main nerve and brain

main blood vessels

Why do people blush ?

Everyone blushes. It's a normal reaction to feeling embarrassed, anxious or excited. It is caused by an increased blood flow through the tiny vessels in the skin of your cheeks. Sometimes people may not blush visibly, but may react differently, like tapping their fingers. Blushing is associated more with young people, rather than old people – and women blush more often than men do.

Close-up of the skin showing a sweat pore, where sweat seeps onto the surface.

What are goose bumps ?

When you are cold or scared, you sometimes develop goose bumps. Goose bumps are temporary bumps on your skin caused by the muscles that pull hairs upright. The body does this when it is cold, as it tries to insulate warm air between the hair, trapping any body heat. Goose bumps serve a purpose in animals, fluffing up fur to make them warmer or to make them look bigger and scarier.

WHAT A NERVE!

Made up of the brain, spinal cord and billions of long nerve cells, the body's nervous system is the most complex and important network in the body. It is essential to seeing, thinking, dreaming, breathing, moving, running, sleeping, laughing, remembering, pain, pleasure, writing ... everything you do!

What is the nervous system

Made up of your brain, your spinal cord and an enormous network of around 30,000 million nerves that thread throughout your entire body, the central nervous system is the control centre of your body. Your brain uses information it receives from your nerves to coordinate all of your actions and reactions. Without it, life as you know it would be impossible.

What are 'pins and needles'

You may get pins and needles if a nerve becomes squashed or has its blood supply cut off. When this happens, the nerve cells can no longer send clear messages to the brain. This can result in the sensation of numbness, tingling or pricking, otherwise known as 'pins and needles'. Move, stretch and rub the affected area to get rid of the funny feeling.

What is a reflex action

Reflex actions occur quickly and automatically to help your body avoid harm. An example of a reflex action is when you touch something hot with your hand and your hand quickly moves away. The response happens quickly because it is ordered by the spinal cord rather than the brain. If the order was to come from the brain, the signals would have to travel further and your reaction would be slower. If the boy in the picture had to rely on his brain to relay reflex information to his hand, he could have hurt himself when he grabbed the hot mug.

How do nerves collect information

Nerves are connected to sensory receptors in the skin. These receptors are able to collect information from the world around us. There are different nerve endings: Ruffini endings are sensitive to stretching of the skin; Merkel's discs send touch information to the brain; Krause end bulbs are sensitive to temperature.

Krause

Ruffini

Merkel

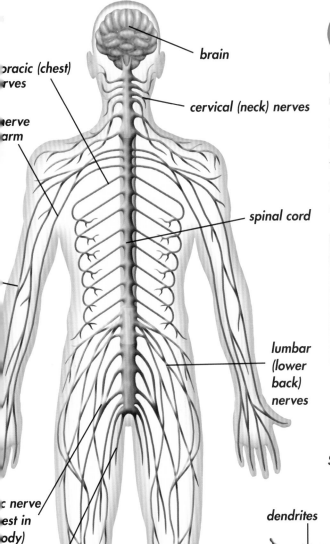

brain

racic (chest)
rves

cervical (neck) nerves

erve
arm

spinal cord

lumbar
(lower
back)
nerves

c nerve
est in
ody)

al nerves

nervous system spreads
gh the whole body.

What is a nerve ?

Nerves, or neurons, are thin threads of cells that run throughout your entire body, carrying messages. Sensory nerves send messages to the brain. They generally connect to the brain through the spinal cord inside your spine. Motor nerves carry messages back from the brain to all the muscles in your body.

slow nerve signal	7.25 km/h
fast nerve signal	362 km/h
sports car	257 km/h
high-speed train	241 km/h

Some nerve signals travel faster than racing cars.

dendrites

axon
(fibre)

dendrites   cell body   nucleus

Nerve cells have shorter branches, called dendrites, to gather signals and a longer one, called the axon, to pass them on.

FACT BYTES

If you lined up all of the neurons in your body, they would stretch for an incredible 950 km!

Every second the nerves transmit nerve signals at speeds of up to 300 km/h, all around the body.

There are more nerve cells in the human brain than there are stars in the Milky Way.

TAKE A DEEP BREATH

The body can survive without water for several days and without food for a week or two – but it can only survive for a few minutes without oxygen. Breathing is one of the body's most vital actions, and we do it almost without thinking – over 20,000 times each day.

Why do we breathe ?

Breathing enables the body to extract the oxygen needed for life and to rid the body of harmful carbon dioxide. Oxygen that comes into the lungs arrives at the alveoli, where it is transferred to the blood. Oxygen is used by the cells in your body to move, build, reproduce and turn food into energy. It is also at the alveoli that carbon dioxide is released from the blood and exhaled from the body.

How many breaths do we take ?

Most people take about 12 to 15 breaths per minute at rest. Each breath moves half a litre of air in and then out of the lungs. After exercise, however, the rate increases to more than 60 breaths each minute, with two litres or more of air each time.

Each breath usually contains half a litre of air.

1 litre

½ litre

0 litre

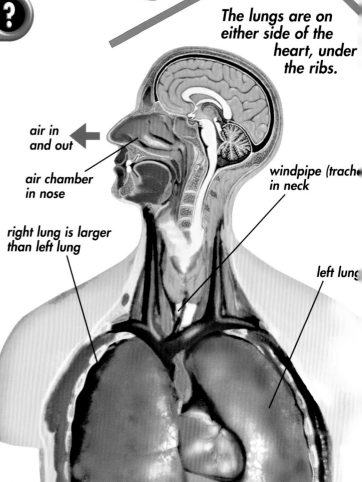

Alveoli are in groups at the ends of the smallest air tubes.

bronchiole

high-oxygen blood back to heart

The lungs are on either side of the heart, under the ribs.

air in and out

air chamber in nose

windpipe (trach in neck

right lung is larger than left lung

left lung

fresh air inside alveolus

tiny blood vessels (capillaries) take up oxygen

What causes hiccups

The diaphragm is a sheet of muscle in your chest, just below your ribcage. When your diaphragm tightens, your lungs expand and you breathe in air. When it loosens, your lungs contract and you breathe out. Hiccups occur when your diaphragm suddenly jerks and air rushes over a flap (epiglottis) at the top of your windpipe, causing it to snap shut. It is the sound of this flap snapping shut that produces the 'hiccup' sound.

air flows into the lungs through the nose or mouth

the flap (epiglottis) snapping shut

full stomach presses upwards

Why do we yawn

Yawning is associated with tiredness, overwork, stress or boredom. However, the specific purpose of yawning is still disputed by scientists. Some think that it cools the brain while others say that it deals with excess carbon dioxide and a lack of oxygen in the body. It could be a way of displaying tiredness or boredom to others. Some scientists think that it is a way of equalising pressure in the ears.

HARD-WORKING HEART

The heart, the blood and the blood vessels make up the human body's cardiovascular system. The heart is responsible for pumping nutrients and gases around the body. The arteries carry blood away from the heart to the body, while the veins carry blood on its return journey back to the heart.

What does the heart do ?

The heart's job is to pump blood around two separate circulations. First it pumps blood rich in oxygen from the lungs around the arteries, delivering food and oxygen to the body. Having delivered its oxygen, the blood then returns to the heart via the veins where it is pumped on its second circuit, this time up to the lungs to pick up more oxygen. The heart is also involved in communication, pumping chemical messages (hormones) around the body.

How does the heart work ?

Blood returns from the lungs through the pulmonary vein. It is delivered to the left atrium, which pushes the blood into the left ventricle. The left ventricle then pushes the blood through the aorta to the rest of the body. The blood returns to the heart through two large veins called the superior and inferior vena cava. It is delivered into the right atrium, which pushes it into the right ventricle. The right ventricle then sends the blood through the pulmonary artery back to the lungs.

main veins from head and upper body

smaller upper chamber (atrium)

heart's left side pumps blood around body

heart's right side pumps blood to lungs

main veins from lower body

How big is the heart ?

The heart is about as big as the clenched fist of its owner. It weighs about 340 g, or about the same as one-and-a-half cans of baked beans. It is positioned higher in the chest than many people think, behind the lower part of the breastbone, and slightly to the left.

FACT BYTES

If all the blood vessels in the body could be joined end to end, they would stretch around the world twice!

main arteries
to head and
arms

main artery
(aorta)

pulmonary
artery to lungs

larger
lower
chamber
(ventricle)

pulmonary
veins from
lungs

coronary
artery

coronary
vein

The heart has
coronary vessels to
supply its own
muscle with blood.

Does the heart ever stop beating

The heart may stop beating while the body is still alive, but only for a very short time. When you sneeze, your lungs are put under great pressure by the squeezing action of chest muscles. The heart is unable to beat properly under this pressure, so it pauses for just a moment.

How fast does the heart beat

Oxygen is pumped around your body in your blood by your heart. Each heartbeat you feel in your chest is one complete contraction and relaxation of the special heart muscle. When you are sitting quietly, your heart beats about 60–80 times a minute. You can count how fast your heart is beating by gently feeling your pulse in your wrist. When you exercise, your heart beats much faster – 120 times or more per minute. This sends more oxygen and energy to the hard-working muscles.

Which are the thickest vessels

The thick-walled arteries and veins that carry blood under pressure to and from the heart are the thickest blood vessels in the body. At any moment, they can contain half of the body's blood. The aorta is the largest artery in the body. It carries blood rich in oxygen from the heart to the other parts of the body. Capillaries are the body's smallest blood vessels. They enable the interchange of water, oxygen, carbon dioxide, nutrients and various waste products between the blood and surrounding tissues.

HARD-WORKING HEART

RED FOR GO!

Every day the heart pumps about 10,000 litres of blood around the body – that's enough to fill 120 bath tubs! The average three-year-old has around 1 litre of blood in their body; the average adult at least five times more!

How much blood is in the body

Blood makes up seven per cent of the body's total weight. For most adults, this makes up about five litres by volume. For the same body size, men have slightly more blood than women, because women have slightly more adipose (fatty) tissues, which need very little blood supply.

Why is blood red

Because it contains red blood cells! So why are they red? They contain a red substance called haemoglobin, which carries vital oxygen from the lungs to be used all around the body. Blood that is rich in oxygen is a brighter shade of red than blood that contains little oxygen. Veins appear blue through the skin due to the interaction of light with the skin and the way that our brain interprets colour.

Red blood cells are doughnut shaped.

What is blood

Your blood is made up of many different cells. Most of your blood is a liquid called plasma. Red blood cells deliver oxygen to the cells in the body and carry back waste gases in exchange. White blood cells are part of your body's defence against disease. Some attack and kill germs eating them up; others attack them with chemicals. Platelets are other cells that help your body repair itself after injury.

How does a cut heal itself

Platelets are the smallest cells in the body. They have one function only: to make blood clot when bleeding has to be stopped! Platelets are small sticky cells that are made in the bone marrow. They rush to the site of a cut, stick to the vessel wall and to each other so that a plug is formed. After this, other substances in the blood work with platelets to form a fibrin, which provides a more permanent solution to bleeding, such as a scab.

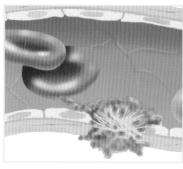
Blood clots to stop bleeding.

otid artery
d jugular
n in neck

hial
y and
to arm

ic
s

*pulmonary
arteries to lungs*

*pulmonary
veins from
lungs*

*aorta
(main
artery
from
heart)*

ral artery
vein in

*posterior tibial
artery and
vein in back
of shin*

or tibial
and
n front
n

**The circulatory
system.**

es
eins

Why do people give blood ?

We give blood because it's very important to
help people who need it. People may need
blood after an accident or during an
operation. Haemophiliacs have a condition
that stops their blood from clotting properly.
They can lose lots of blood very quickly if
they are cut, so often require blood
transfusions to keep them healthy. It's also
important to check the pumping force of the
heart, called blood pressure, with a blood
pressure cuff around the arm.

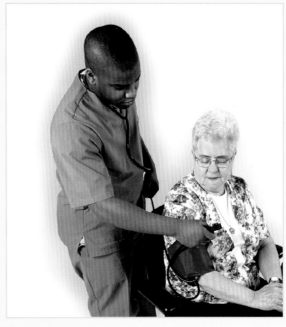

What are blood groups ?

People with different blood groups have different
substances in their blood. If a person needs a
blood donation, or transfusion, blood of a suitable
group is chosen – the wrong type could be deadly.
Most people are blood type O. Next comes A,
then B, with only one person in 20 being type AB.

RED FOR GO!

FUELLING THE BODY

The digestive system is made up of a variety of different organs and substances that work together to break down food into nutrients and energy that can be absorbed and used in the body's tissues and cells.

Why do we feel hungry

The body uses energy all the time, not only to move about, speak and eat, but also to make the heart beat, the lungs breathe and for many other internal processes. As stores of energy gradually decrease, the body signals the need for more energy by making us feel hungry.

How does food reach the stomach

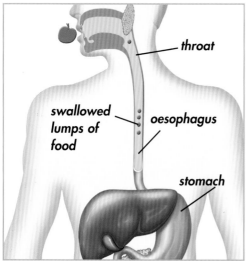

throat

swallowed lumps of food

oesophagus

stomach

The oesophagus carries food through the chest.

After food has been chewed in the mouth, it travels down the oesophagus and into the stomach. The oesophagus is a 25 cm long, muscular tube that contracts in waves to move swallowed food through it. The swallowing sound that can be heard during eating is the sound of the oesophagus functioning.

liver

gall bladder

What are the 'guts'

This is a general name for the intestines and the stomach too. The stomach is a J-shaped bag which receives swallowed foods and drinks. It squeezes, mashes and mixes food with powerful juices, including strong acids and digestive enzymes. From the stomach, food passes into the very long, coiled small intestine, where the digested nutrients are taken into the body. The leftovers go on, into the shorter but wider large intestine, which takes in water and a few more nutrients. The whole process leaves faeces at the end, in the rectum, ready to be removed from the body.

The digestive system is mainly in the lower body or abdomen.

oesophagus

stomach

pancreas (makes digestive juices)

large intestine (colon)

coils and loops of small intestine (ileum)

rectum

Why does it take longer to digest a carrot than a cake ?

The time for digestion depends on the type of food. Sugary and starchy foods like cakes break down quite quickly in the stomach and contain plenty of energy. Fruits and vegetables need more chewing and mashing. Fatty meals, especially those with lots of animal fats, take longest to digest.

A diet should be varied and healthy.

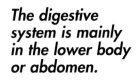

Carbohydrates include bread, pasta, cereal and rice.

Vitamins and minerals are found in fruit and vegetables.

Proteins include fish, eggs and red meat.

Fatty foods include cheese and milk.

Why do people vomit ?

The muscles of the oesophagus wall are so powerful, a person could swallow while upside down. They work in reverse too, to remove bad or unwanted food from the stomach, up and out of the mouth – by vomiting!

FACT BYTES

The whole digestive tract is about 8–9 m long.
Mouth and throat 20 cm
Oesophagus 25 cm
Stomach 25 cm
Small intestine 600 cm
Large intestine 150 cm
Rectum 15 cm

WASTE!

Excretion is the process of ridding the body of waste products that must be removed if the body is to remain healthy. The body relies on various organs for waste removal, including the kidneys, the lungs, the liver, the bladder and the intestines.

Why do people go to the toilet ?

We go to the toilet to rid the body of unwanted waste products. Faeces (poo!) is made up of undigested and leftover food, bits of old lining from the digestive system and old red blood cells from the liver. About 75 per cent of its weight is water, and about 10 per cent is dead gut bacteria. These bacteria live in their millions in the large intestine and help with digestion. Produced by the kidneys, urine contains waste products produced by the body's billions of cells.

renal artery and vein for blood supply

Why are faeces different colours ?

The colour of faeces depends on the foods we eat. Lots of fatty foods makes them pale. Plenty of iron-rich foods make them darker. If there is not enough fibre in food, from fruits and vegetables, the faeces may be too small and hard. They get stuck on the way out, which is known as constipation.

pipe to bladder (ureter)

Greens and red meat are rich in iron and make faeces darker.

What do the kidneys do ?

The kidneys collect and filter waste products from the blood. They also control the amount of water passed out of the body, and maintain the body's balance of salt. From the kidneys, waste products and excess water are passed in the form of urine down to the bladder, before they are passed out of the body. The kidneys filter about one litre of blood every minute. They produce urine continuously during the day and night. The body passes about two litres of urine every single day!

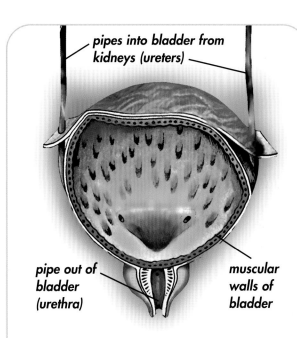

pipes into bladder from kidneys (ureters)

pipe out of bladder (urethra)

muscular walls of bladder

The bladder is a stretchy bag for urine.

urine collects in central area

main part of kidney contains over one million micro-filters

Cross section of a kidney.

FACT BYTES

The kidneys receive more blood, for their size, than any other body part – about 20 per cent of all the blood pumped out from the heart.

Each day the kidneys filter the body's entire volume of blood more than 300 times.

Food drying up in the large intestine can remain there for eight hours to two days!

WASTE!

GET A GRIP

The hand is one of the most useful parts of the human body. From gripping a tennis racket to threading a needle, our hands are perfectly designed for performing everyday activities in the world around us.

How do hands work

The hand is truly amazing. It allows us to grip, hold, clench and perform more delicate movements like writing. It is operated by more than 50 muscles – the thumb alone has about ten muscles that move and bend it in almost every direction! Most of your hand-moving muscles are joined to bones by long, cord-like tendons that pass through the wrist. Clench your hand and you can see these tendons moving in your wrist!

blood vessels run to skin and bone of fingertip

How do hands 'talk'

We communicate with our hands and fingers in many ways. For example, the forefinger held to the lips means, 'Shhhh – keep quiet'. A fist clenched by the cheek, with the thumb to the ear and the little finger to the lips, means 'I'm on the telephone.' Hands can 'talk' in another way too – by sign language. This is especially useful for people who cannot hear properly.

How many bones are in the hand

The hand has 27 bones. There are five in the palm, called metacarpals, two bones in the thumb and three in each finger, all known as phalanges. There are also eight small bones, called carpals, in the wrist, which join the hand to the forearm bones.

The digits are numbered 1 (thumb) to 5 (little finger).

digit 3 (middle finger)

distal phalanx

middle phalanx

proximal phalanx

carpal bones in wrist

metacarpal bone in palm

digit 1 (thumb)

abductor minimi pulls little finger over palm

main ulnar nerve

Why do we have fingerprints

The pattern of small, curved ridges in the fingertips help fingers to grip. Smooth skin would grip much more poorly. The fingertip skin also has a thin film of sweat to improve the grip further. It's not exactly clear why everyone should have different patterns, but as no print is the same they are helpful for identifying people.

arch

tented arch

pocket loop

whorl

tendons of finger muscles run to fingertip

ligaments criss-cross over tendons

distal phalanx bone of thumb

nerves run to skin of thumb tip

abductor pollicis pulls thumb towards palm

tendons run under carpal ligament in wrist

tendons from finger-curling muscles in forearm

Dozens of muscles make the fingers move.

Why is the thumb so useful

Because it can 'oppose' each finger, which means it can touch and press against each finger in turn. This gives a type of grip, called the 'power grip', between the side of the thumb and all the fingers, which is used for holding objects tightly. The 'precision grip' is between the end of the thumb and a fingertip, to hold small items.

The power grip is used to grasp items tightly, like this tennis racquet.

GET A GRIP

BEST FOOT FORWARD

Your feet are incredibly sturdy, strong and flexible. They are able to support the weight of your entire body and still perform delicate movements like wiggling your toes. Your toenails are designed to aid balance, and the skin on the sole is the thickest of any on the human body.

How many bones are in the foot ?

There are 26 bones in the foot – five in the sole, two in the big toe, and three in each of the other four toes. There are also seven bones in the ankle. One of these, called the calcaneus, forms the rear of the foot and the heel. Strangely, the knobbly parts we call the ankles, on the inside and outside of the ankle joint, are not ankle bones – in fact, they are the lower ends of the long bones, called the tibia and fibula, inside the leg.

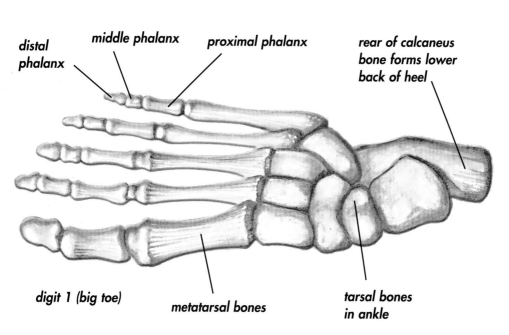

gastrocnemius muscle in calf

main shinbone (tibia)

tendons run under strap-like tarsal ligament in front of ankle

flexor hallucis muscle curls big toe downwards

tendons attach to toe bones

distal phalanx

middle phalanx

proximal phalanx

rear of calcaneus bone forms lower back of heel

digit 1 (big toe)

metatarsal bones

tarsal bones in ankle

muscle sheaths around muscles of big toe

extensor tendon pulling toe up runs to tip of big toe

Why do men have bigger feet than women ?

Partly because, on average, men have larger bodies than women. However, that is not the only reason. The male hormone testosterone has an effect on bone growth and makes parts such as the nose, chin, hands and feet grow more during the teenage years in boys. No human being is perfectly symmetrical, and most of us have one foot bigger than the other.

The foot and ankle are worked by many muscles in the shin.

calf bone (fibula)

outer ankle is lower end of fibula bone

tendons of toe-curling shin muscles

nerves control toe muscles and feelings from skin

interossei muscles connect bones of toes

How much pressure does the foot have to absorb

With every step you take, your feet have to absorb a pressure that is about one and a half times the weight of your body. If you run or jump, the force may be many times your body weight. You can see how the pressure varies during slow walking, jogging and leaping; just look at the depth of the different parts of a footprint in damp mud or sand.

walking   jogging   running

Running will leave the deepest footprints.

FACT BYTES

Some people who lose the use of their hands, for example, in an accident, can learn to use their feet and toes instead for many actions – from typing at a computer to painting pictures.

Each foot is able to take up to five times your body weight when running.

Using their nails helped our ancestors grip more easily with their toes.

Why do we have toenails

Some scientists think that toenails aid walking, by making the toes stronger and stiffer for a better grip on the ground. Long ago, when our distant ape-like ancestors lived in trees, their toes were as good at holding and gripping branches as their hands. Toenails may also be involved in balance and coordination.

BEST FOOT FORWARD

EXPECTING A BABY

Everyone begins life in the same way – as a tiny fertilised egg, smaller than the full stop at the end of this sentence. The development of a baby in the mother's womb is one of the most amazing parts of the human life cycle.

After nine months in the womb the baby is head-down, ready to be born.

How long does a baby spend in the womb ❓

Even though a baby is thought of as age 'nought' or 'zero' when it is born, at birth it is already nine months old – this is the length of time spent developing in its mother's womb during pregnancy.

How does life begin ❓

Life begins with a fertilised egg, or embryo. This involves the coming together of two cells. One is the egg cell, produced inside the mother's sex organs, or ovaries. Each month one of them becomes larger and ripe, and an egg is released

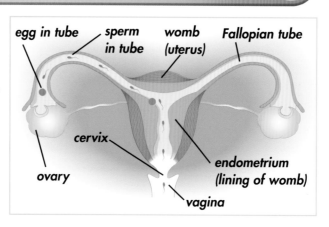

egg in tube — sperm in tube — womb (uterus) — Fallopian tube

cervix

ovary

endometrium (lining of womb)

vagina

into the Fallopian tube (oviduct). Here it may meet the other cell, a sperm cell, which comes from the father. Sperm are made in the male sex organs, or testes. When egg and sperm join, it is called fertilisation.

What is an embryo ❓

smaller cells around the embryo

the fertilised egg has divided into two cells

A two-cell embryo.

The embryo stage is from fertilisation to eight weeks later. The fertilised egg moves along the Fallopian tube into the womb, where it sinks into the blood-rich lining. All the time it is dividing and re-dividing to form a small group of cells called the merula. By eight weeks this group of cells has developed to form the main parts of the human body, yet the curled-up embryo is hardly larger than a grape.

6 weeks

12 weeks

16 weeks

What is a foetus ?

Supply of nutrients from the mother's blood.

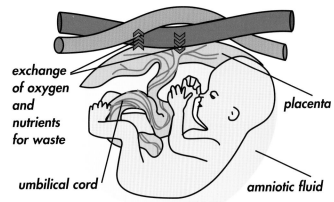

exchange
of oxygen
and
nutrients
for waste

placenta

umbilical cord

amniotic fluid

After eight weeks, the embryo is called a foetus. It continues to grow fast as smaller details of its body form, like eyelids and fingernails. By the time of birth (depending on the parents' size and ethnic group) the baby weighs about 3–3.5 kg.

How does a baby breathe in the womb ?

It can't – it is surrounded by fluid in the womb! The foetus receives all the oxygen it needs from its mother. This vital exchange is carried out by the placenta, to which the foetus is attached by the umbilical cord. At the placenta, the foetus's blood vessels pass closely to the mother's blood vessels and the exchange of oxygen, food and waste products takes place. The placenta also acts as a barrier to protect the foetus from harmful substances.

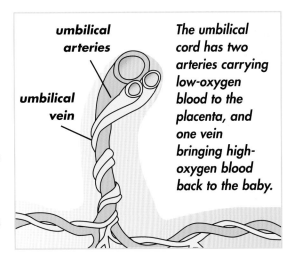

umbilical
arteries

umbilical
vein

The umbilical cord has two arteries carrying low-oxygen blood to the placenta, and one vein bringing high-oxygen blood back to the baby.

20 weeks

28 weeks

38 weeks

FACT BYTES

Throughout a woman's lifetime, she will produce 400–500 egg cells.

The human heart starts to beat 21 days after conception.

From fertilised egg to full-grown foetus, body weight increases six billion (6,000,000,000) times!

EXPECTING A BABY

A NEW LIFE BEGINS

A baby spends about 38-40 weeks growing inside its mother's womb (uterus), where it is warm, dark, well fed and protected. The lights, sounds, actions and fresh air of birth come as a big shock!

How is a baby born

The womb in which the baby grows has powerful muscles in its walls, and a narrow, pocket-like opening called the cervix. At birth, the womb muscles shorten or contract powerfully, and the cervix becomes much wider. The muscles push the baby through the dilated cervix, along a tunnel called the vagina, or birth canal, and out of the mother's body.

How long does birth take

On average, it takes 14–17 hours for a mother to deliver her first baby, much shorter for her second baby, even shorter for the third, and so on. The longest part of birth is the first stage when the womb muscles start to contract. These muscle contractions can last for a number of days. The second stage, delivery, is when the baby moves along the birth canal and emerges. The third stage, afterbirth, is when the placenta also leaves the womb.

The womb muscles contract.

- womb
- pubic bone
- vagina
- cervix
- spine
- spinal cord

Moving into the birth canal.

- cervix dilates (widens)

muscles in wall of womb

The baby's head presses down on the cervix (womb opening) at the start of birth.

When are most babies born

Through the months of the year, slightly more babies than normal are born during August, and slightly fewer in April. The most common time of 'day' for births is actually the middle of the night, between 3 and 4 am. The least common is twelve hours later, around 3 pm in the afternoon.

FACT BYTES

For every 100 new baby girls, on average, there are 105 new baby boys.

At the time of birth, the womb (uterus) contains the most powerful muscles in the human body – 40 times their size before pregnancy.

cervix is
ready to
open

What colour are a baby's eyes ?

Nearly all babies have grey-blue eyes at birth. This is because the coloured part of the eye, the iris, has not yet developed its full set of microscopic cells which produce the colouring substance, or pigment. The eventual colour develops over a few months.

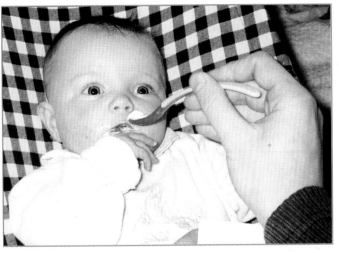

A blue-eyed new baby stares at the bright world.

A baby feeds.

What is a baby's first food ?

Mother's milk is the perfect food for new babies. It contains all the nutrients, fluids and energy that the baby needs, and it is clean, freshly made, and readily available, straight from the mother's breast. Some mothers are unable to make milk, produce too little, or become ill. For these and other reasons, powder or formula milk can be used.

BABIES AND TODDLERS

During the first years of life, a child develops rapidly and learns a great deal about social roles and behaviour. It is during this time that they learn to walk and talk. Young children are like little sponges, soaking up information about the world around them.

When does a baby first smile

On average, from about six weeks. Smiling is an important part of communication. A smile can indicate that a baby is happy and content, or wants attention of some kind. Long before the first smile, babies want to communicate with people, by holding the gaze of others and then widening their eyes or moving the tongue.

Can toddlers walk before they crawl

Most babies and toddlers go through the stages of development in the same order, but their age at each stage can differ greatly. A typical youngster rolls over at nine to ten weeks of age, sits up unaided at eighteen to twenty weeks, tries to stand up supported from six or seven months, and crawls at eight months. He or she may walk unaided at eleven to twelve months.

Some babies don't bother with crawling. They learn to roll sideways or bottom-shuffle, and then go straight to walking.

Sitting and standing are important stages, or 'milestones', of development.

Why do toddlers like bland foods ?

Our sense of taste helps to warn of foods which are bad, rotten, 'gone off' or poisonous – and these often taste sour or bitter. A toddler follows their in-built reactions, or instincts, and avoids these tastes. Gradually, as the toddler grows into a child and experiences more flavours, he or she learns to tell apart different tastes and knows which foods may be rotten or bad in some way.

Babies don't eat food – they wear it!

What does cutting teeth mean ?

Between seven and twelve months, teeth start to grow and push through the baby's mouth. They come from little tooth 'buds' which were formed whilst in the womb. Usually, the first to appear are the 'central' incisors, or front teeth, followed by the 'lateral' incisors. The baby is likely to drool more, eat and sleep less and be generally uncomfortable – which is not surprising! Most babies have a full set of milk teeth at three years. By the time they are six, they start to lose them as the permanent teeth come through.

molars
lateral incisor
central incisor
canine

FACT BYTES

A baby grows fastest as a foetus and through the first two years of life.

From the age of two, both boys and girls grow about seven or eight centimetres a year, with boys typically being slightly taller.

Is it true that newborn babies can swim ?

Having spent months suspended in fluid in their mother's womb, babies feel at home in the water. All babies are born with a swim and dive reflex. This means that they automatically hold their breath under water and are able to swim for short distances. This reflex is strongest when a baby is under three months old. After this time babies can develop a fear of the water – but they can easily learn to swim properly when they are older.

BABIES AND TODDLERS

GROWING OLDER

Growing 'up' is not just getting taller, or even becoming bigger all over. It means a whole host of changes inside the body, especially during the teenage years. As many more years go by, things change again and bodily systems start to slow down.

What is puberty

Puberty is the time when the sex organs (reproductive parts) become active and start to function. This phase mainly involves physical growth and development. Puberty is part of a longer period called adolescence, which involves many mental and emotional changes, changes in friendships and social life, and increasing independence from parents.

What is the menstrual cycle

The menstrual cycle is something that is necessary for reproduction. During the menstrual cycle, the ovary releases an egg in an event called ovulation. If the egg is not fertilised it will die and be absorbed by the woman's body. After this, hormones cause the uterus to shed its lining in a process called menstruation.

Adolescent boy and girl.

egg matures in ovary   ovulation (egg released from ovary)   egg breaks down

womb lining is shed (menstruation)   level of oestrogen

end of menstruation

level of progesterone

| 1 day | 7 days | 14 days | 21 days | 28 days |

start of menstruation

The menstrual cycle lasts on average 28 days.

When do women stop having babies

The menstrual cycles of women usually stop around the age of 50–55 years. This stage of life is called the menopause, and it means that eggs are no longer produced by the ovaries. However, with modern medical techniques such as IVF (in vitro fertilisation or 'test tube babies'), it has become possible for women to conceive at a much later age. Most men carry on making sperm for longer, into their 60s or even 70s, so they can still be fathers.

Why do voices 'break'

The bodily changes of puberty involve extra growth of the voice box, or larynx, in the neck. The strip-like vocal folds (cords), which vibrate to make the sound of the voice, become thicker and stiffer. They vibrate more slowly, making the voice deeper. This happens most noticeably in boys, whose voices 'break' or 'crack' during puberty, but also to an extent in girls.

hyoid bone

epiglottis

thyroid cartilage

vocal cords inside voice box

cricoid cartilage

windpipe (trachea)

The voice box grows during puberty.

Why does skin become wrinkly

Skin contains tiny threads, or fibres, of the substance elastin. Like millions of microscopic elastic bands, these make the skin spring back after it is stretched. With age, the amount of elastin becomes less so the skin becomes stretched and loose, and puckers into creases and wrinkles.

GROWING OLDER

EAT WELL, STAY FIT!

The body benefits from moderate and regular exercise, two or three times weekly, and also a wide range of foods and drink. The body needs a well-balanced diet to provide it with the substances it requires for energy, growth and repair.

Which foods are healthy

Fresh fruits are very healthy.

The body can cope with most kinds of food. The main problem is too much of any one kind, whether it's crisps or carrots. A varied diet is best. Fresh fruits and vegetables are especially healthy. Most people benefit from four or five portions of them daily – a portion being a piece of fruit (like a banana or apple) or a helping of vegetables.

Which foods aren't healthy

Too many fatty foods can be bad for the body, especially foods with lots of animal fats such as fatty meats or full-fat cheeses. In particular, they affect the heart and blood vessels. Also, too much food in total is unhealthy. Being overweight or obese increases the risk of many problems such as heart disease, high blood pressure, muscle and joint problems, breathlessness, diabetes, and breathing and lung disorders.

Fatty and fried foods can lead to serious heart problems.

Why is smoking harmful ?

Smoking tobacco is a very bad idea. It is linked with diseases such as heart disease and cancers of the lungs, throat, gullet, bladder and many other parts. It can cause breathlessness, wheezing and increased risk of infections such as bronchitis and pneumonia. Worldwide, there were about 100 million tobacco deaths during the twentieth century alone.

Regular exercise benefits all parts of the body.

Which sport or exercise is best ?

The type of exercise or activity does not matter too much, provided it is done in moderation.

We are more likely to continue with regular exercise if:

• We enjoy it and it's good fun.
• It fits in with our daily or weekly routine.
• It doesn't involve too much special equipment, travel or money.

It could be a team game like football or hockey, a sport such as tennis or squash, or swimming, cycling, rowing, jogging, horse riding ... the choices are endless.

Swimming is a great way to get fit.

How often should we take exercise ?

Most people benefit from at least two exercise sessions each week. These should be enough to cause faster breathing and more rapid pulse rate, which shows the lungs and heart are getting a workout. A bit of sweat is also usually a good sign.

EAT WELL, STAY FIT!

GLOSSARY

Achilles tendon
The fibrous cord that connects the calf muscles to the heel bone.

Alveoli
Tiny air sacs in the lungs that carry the oxygen from the air into the blood.

Canines
The taller, pointed teeth to the sides of the incisors at the front of the mouth, good for tearing tough food.

Capillary
Delicate, thin-walled blood vessels, some of which are finer than human hairs.

Carbohydrate
One of the main food groups, relatively high in sugar and starch – includes bread and potatoes.

Carpals
The eight small bones of the wrist which join the hand to the forearm bones.

Cartilage
A tough, relatively flexible tissue that can be found in the nose and ears and in joints – most of the skeleton is made from harder bone.

Cell
The smallest unit of an organism (living thing) that can function on its own.

Cerebellum
The part of the brain that coordinates movement and balance.

Cerumen
Ear wax that plays an important role in cleaning the ear canal.

Cilia
Tiny hairs on cells, such as those in the nose that, when touched by odorants, send messages to the brain for our sense of smell.

DNA
Deoxyribonucleic acid – the chemical substance that carries genetic information.

EEG
An EEG, or electro-encephalograph, is an instrument that records the electrical activity of the brain by means of electrodes placed on the scalp.

Enamel
The hard, white substance that covers each tooth.

Eustachian tube
A tube inside the ear which acts as a pressure gauge, letting air both in and out.

Fertilisation
The point at which the man's sperm joins with the woman's egg and the life of a baby starts.

Fibrin
A protein formed when blood clots, making a network that holds the red blood cells and platelets together.

Fibrous
Consisting of, or resembling, fibres, as in fibrous tissue.

Foetus
The tiny, growing baby in the womb, from the second month of pregnancy.

Fontanelle
A small gap in the top of a baby's skull which can appear as a soft spot.

Genes
Inherited genes carry instructions for how the body grows and develops and carries out life processes.

Habituation
The way in which the body gets used to how it receives the various senses of smell, touch, hearing, sight and taste.

Haemoglobin
A protein that gives the red colour to blood cells.

Hair follicle
A tiny cavity in the skin from which hair grows. It houses the only part of the hair which is alive.

Hormone
A chemical substance that carries a signal from one cell to another. Produced in the endocrine glands, it is transported in the blood.

Incisors
The chisel-edged teeth at the front of the mouth.

IVF
In Vitro Fertilisation – if a woman is unable to conceive naturally, egg cells can be removed from the woman's ovary and fertilised by the sperm outside the body, before being implanted in her womb (uterus) when pregnancy proceeds in the normal way.

Keratin
The substance (a protein) from which nails and hair are made.

Melanin
A group of black or dark brown pigments in the hair, skin and eyes of humans.

Metacarpals
The five bones that form the palm of the hand.

Myofibril
Muscle fibre that consists of actin and myosin proteins.

Nerve
A fibre in the body that transmits messages between the brain or spinal cord and other parts of the body.

Nutrient
Any substance that nourishes the body – repairing it when needed and keeping it in good working order.

Odorant
A 'smelly' airborne particle that floats into the air and into our nose, touching micro-hairs (cilia) which give us the sense of smell.

Oestrogen
A hormone which produces and maintains female characteristics.

Ossicles
The three tiny bones of the inner ear, known as the malleus (hammer), incus (anvil) and stapes (stirrup).

Paresthesia
The medical term given to 'pins and needles' – a loss of sensation in areas where the blood pressure has been affected.

Phalanges
The two bones of each thumb and three bones of each finger.

Pigment
A substance that is found in animal or plant tissue that produces the dominant colour.

Plasma
The yellowish, clear fluid part of the blood.

Platelet
A minute particle in the blood which helps it to clot.

Receptor
A nerve ending which responds to touch and sends messages to the brain, for example, touching a hot surface with our fingertips and then moving them quickly away.

Retina
The light-sensitive lining at the back of the eyeball.

Sebaceous gland
Small glands in the skin that secrete sebum into the hair follicles and over the surface of the body – except the soles of the feet and the palms of the hands.

Sound waves
Waves that enable sound to travel, as in the sound travelling from the mouth through the air to our ears.

Synovial fluid
A clear, lubricating fluid secreted by the membrane lining the joints, making joint movement smooth.

Testosterone
A very strong hormone produced by the testes in the male.

Umbilical cord
The long, tube-shaped cord joining the foetus to the placenta, along which vital nutrients are passed from the mother.

UV rays
Ultra-violet rays from the Sun which can cause wrinkles and premature aging as well as sunburn.

Vena cava
The two large veins that carry oxygen-depleted blood to the heart.

GLOSSARY

INDEX

Acknowledgements

Main illustrations by Pulsar Estudio/Meme Design.

Key:Top - t; middle - m; bottom - b; left - l; right - r;

Front and back cover: stephen Sweet/SGA.
1: Meme Design. **2-4:** Meme Design. **5:** (t, b) Meme Design; (m) TT. **6-7:** Meme Design. **8:** (ml) SGA; (r) Meme Design. **9:** (tr) Meme Design; (br) Beehive Illustration. **10:** (m, mr) Meme Design; (b) TTAT. **11:** (t) TT; (b) Meme Design. **12:** (tr) Stephen Sweet/SGA; (b) Meme Design. **13:** (tr) TT; (br) Beehive Illustrations. **14:** Meme Design. **15:** (ml) stephen Sweet/SGA; (t) SGA; (m,b) Meme Design. **16:** (ml) SGA. **17:** (l) Meme Design; (mr, br) Stephen Sweet/SGA. **18:** (ml,br) Photodisc; (bl) Meme Design. **19:** (l) Meme Design; (mr, br) TTAT. **20:** (bl) TT; (m) Meme Design; (r) Stephen Sweet/SGA. **21:** (l) Stephen Sweet/SGA; (mr) Meme Design. **22:** (tr) Beehive Illustrations; (bl) Meme Design. **23:** (tr) stephen Sweet/SGA; (bl) Meme Design; (br) TT. **24:** (ml) Stephen Sweet/SGA; (mr, br) Meme Design. **25:** (br) Susumu Nishinaga/Science Photo Library. **26:** (ml) TT; (r) Stephen Sweet/SGA. **27:** (tr, m) Meme Design. **28:** Meme Design. **29:** Meme Design. **30:** (bl) Meme Design. **31:** (l) Stephen Sweet/SGA; (mr)